MY GUINEA PIG

Me and My PET

By William Anthony

KidHaven PUBLISHING

Published in 2020 by KidHaven Publishing, an Imprint of Greenhaven Publishing, LLC
353 3rd Avenue, Suite 255, New York, NY 10010

This edition is published by arrangement with Booklife Publishing.

Written by: William Anthony
Edited by: Madeline Tyler
Designed by: Jasmine Pointer

Cataloging-in-Publication Data

Names: Anthony, William.
Title: My guinea pig / William Anthony.
Description: New York : KidHaven Publishing, 2020. | Series: Me and my pet | Includes glossary and index.
Identifiers: ISBN 9781534533455 (pbk.) | ISBN 9781534533479 (library bound) | ISBN 9781534533462 (6 pack) | ISBN 9781534533486 (ebook)
Subjects: LCSH: Guinea pigs as pets--Juvenile literature.
Classification: LCC SF459.G9 A58 2020 | DDC 636.935'92--dc23

Photo credits: Images are courtesy of Shutterstock.com. With thanks to Getty Images, Thinkstock Photo and iStockphoto.
Front cover - Tatyana Vyc; Winning7799. 2 - StineMah. 3 - Vasily Kovalev, Africa Studio. 4 - In Green. 5 - Tatyana Vyc. 6 - Daisy Daisy. 7 - Tatyana
Vyc. 8 - Dantyya. 9 - CatJB. 10 - JohnatAPW, Tim Large. 11 - Heder Zambrano. 12 - Fangfy. 13 - yurilily. 14 & 15 - Shchus. 16 - Monkey Business
Images. 17 - Tatyana Vyc. 18 - Chertamchu. 19 - DmitryPron. 20 - Dev_Maryna. 21 - Eric Isselee. 22 - Tatyana Vyc. 23 - Djem.

Printed in the United States of America

CPSIA compliance information: Batch #BW20KL: For further information contact Greenhaven Publishing LLC, New York, New York at 1-844-317-7404.

CONTENTS

Page 4 — Zoe and Fudge

Page 6 — Getting Guinea Pigs

Page 8 — Home

Page 10 — Playtime

Page 12 — Food

Page 14 — Bedtime

Page 16 — The Vet

Page 18 — Growing Up

Page 20 — Super Guinea Pigs

Page 22 — You and Your Pet

Page 24 — Glossary and Index

Words that look like this can be found in the glossary on page 24.

Zoe ♥ and Fudge

Zoe

Hello! My name's Zoe, and this is my pet guinea pig, Fudge. He's four years old. He has a friend called Sherbet. They live together because guinea pigs like living in **pairs**!

Fudge

I think Sherbet's sleeping at the moment, so it looks like it will be just me and Fudge talking you through how to look after guinea pigs!

Lead the way, Fudge!

Getting Guinea Pigs

Looking after guinea pigs means you are going to have a lot of <u>responsibility</u>. You will need to feed them and give them a nice home with lots of space.

My family got Fudge and Sherbet from a pet store, but you can also get guinea pigs from a rescue center or from a breeder. A breeder is someone who keeps guinea pigs to mate them.

Remember, it's best to keep guinea pigs in pairs, so be ready to look after two animals!

Home

If you keep your guinea pig outside, make sure their home is warm and out of the wind.

Guinea pigs don't like loud noises. If your house is noisy, it might be a good idea to keep them outside.

They will need a cage with lots of space for exercise and a good shelter where they can sleep. You could get them tunnels for their cage to keep them entertained.

Playtime

Guinea Pig Run

Most guinea pigs have fun exploring.
You could also get them a **run** so they
can explore safely in your garden.

10

When you're playing with your guinea pigs, you must be very calm and gentle. Since guinea pigs don't like loud noises, don't shout when you're petting them.

Food

Guinea pigs need food to stay alive, just like us. They are easy animals to feed. Guinea pigs need lots of hay and some pellet food, which you can get from any pet store.

Pellet Food

Guinea pigs need different types of food in their <u>diet</u>.

You can also give your guinea pigs different types of vegetables. They like things like carrots, broccoli, and cabbage. This keeps their diet healthy and <u>balanced</u>.

Bedtime zzᶻ

Sherbet is still asleep. Shall we take a quick peek?
He's sleeping on a soft and fluffy blanket. Guinea pigs
also like to sleep on soft paper or wood shavings.

Sorry, Sherbet, did we wake you up? We'll move on and let you get back to sleep! Guinea pigs usually have short naps, so he'll be awake again soon.

The Vet

Vets are doctors, but for animals instead of humans!

Guinea pigs can get sick, just like humans. Guinea pigs that are sick can go to the vet. The vet will do everything they can to help your guinea pig get better again!

One day when I came home, Fudge was sneezing and had crusty eyes. I told my parents and we took him to the vet, who made him all better again!

If you think your guinea pig isn't well, make sure you tell an adult.

Growing Up

When guinea pigs get older, they find it hard to move as quickly as they used to. It's important to be gentle with older guinea pigs.

You could also try to make their cage more comfortable. Make sure they can reach their water easily, and have somewhere soft to rest and sleep.

You could even bring your elderly guinea pig indoors to help them stay warm.

Super Guinea Pigs

Normal guinea pigs are amazing, but some guinea pigs are simply super. A guinea pig named Truffles holds the world record for the farthest jump by a guinea pig. He jumped 19 inches (48 cm)!

That's farther than these two pages of this book!

Wow!

ZOOM!

Another guinea pig, named Flash, holds the world record for the fastest 10-meter run. He ran it in just under nine seconds!

You and Your Pet

Whether you have a young guinea pig, an old guinea pig, or a super guinea pig, make sure you take care of them just like Fudge and I have taught you!

I'm sure you'll make a great pet owner. I hope your new furry friend enjoys their new home, and that you have lots of fun together.

GLOSSARY

balanced	having good or equal amounts of something
diet	the kind of food that an animal or person usually eats
mate	to produce young with an animal of the same species
pair	two of something
rescue center	a place that helps animals that have had a difficult life find a new home
responsibility	having tasks that you are expected to do
run	a safe enclosure that lets animals explore different areas while staying safe
shelter	something that covers or protects people or things

INDEX

cage 9, 19
exercise 9
exploring 10
garden 10
gentle 11, 18

hay 12
noises 8, 11
old 4, 18–19, 22
pairs 4, 7
pet store 7, 12

sleep 5, 9, 14–15, 19
vegetables 13
water 19

24